Holiday Crafts

By Anna Suid
Poems by Murray Suid
Illustrated by Susan True

To Mom and Dad, Tanya, Philip, Don,
and teachers everywhere,
For all you do, this book's for you.

THE Author

Publisher: Roberta Suid
Editor: Carol Whiteley
Design and Production: Susan True
Cover art: Corbin Hillam

Entire contents copyright © 1985 by Monday Morning
Books, Inc., Box 1680, Palo Alto, California 94302

ISBN 0-912107-31-6

Printed in the United States of America

9 8 7 6 5 4 3 2 1

Introduction

In *Holiday Crafts,* you'll find over 50 easy-to-do projects for teaching and celebrating Halloween, St. Patrick's Day, Thanksgiving, and eight other festivals. Each carefully tested activity uses readily available and inexpensive materials. Because the crafts require only limited adult supervision, there is plenty of room for children to let their imaginations run free. While older children may turn out more elaborate work, even the youngest "craftsperson" will produce delightful and valuable finished products.

Holidays can offer surprising opportunities for play, invention, problem-solving, and sharing. This book shows how to turn these possibilities into memorable events for children ages three to six. . .and for you, too.

An original poem sets the stage for each holiday. Most of these short verses are easy to memorize. Children can present or teach the rhymes to friends, neighbors, and relatives.

I hope the book brings hours of joy to teachers, parents, and children everywhere.

HAPPY HOLIDAYS!

Contents

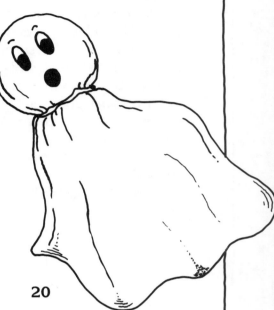

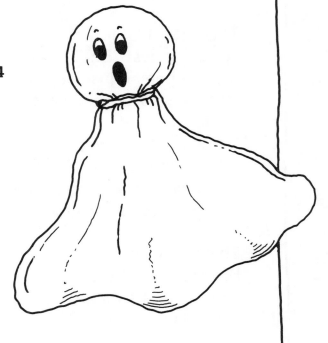

Halloween

Why Real Ghosts Hate Halloween

Who says it's easy
Being a ghost?
You'd find the job tricky,
Much harder than most.

It's never simple
When you've got to be mean.
But the worst time, believe me,
Is called Halloween.

At each home kids visit,
They call, "Trick or treat,"
Hoping to scare up
A sweet thing to eat.

Then later I try it.
I give my best "Boo!"
But the person just laughs
And asks, "Whose kid are you?"

"I'm no kid," I howl,
"Now hand over the food."
"No way," comes the answer,
"Because you're too rude."

That's why I do hate
Halloween, as I said.
All real ghosts that night
Might as well stay in bed.

Envelope Ghost Puppet

You Will Need:
envelope
scissors
pen

What You Do:
1. Seal the envelope.
2. Draw a ghost lengthwise on the envelope. He can just be a flat-bottomed oval with two circles for eyes.
3. Cut off the bottom edge of the envelope.
4. Put the ghost puppet on your hand and go scare somebody.

add face

cut off bottom edge

seal envelope

Ghost Lolly

You Will Need:
lollypop
tissue paper
non-toxic felt-tip pen
yarn
scissors

What You Do:
1. Cut out a circle of tissue paper with a diameter about two times the length of the lollypop stick.
2. Wrap the tissue around the lolly and tie its neck with yarn.
3. Draw scary eyes on the tissue with the felt pen.
4. Present your ghostly lolly to the ghoul of your choice!

cut circle out of tissue

wrap yarn and tie →

Jack-o-Orange

You Will Need:
orange
cloves

What You Do:
1. Look at your orange and decide which side you are going to put the face on.
2. Stick the cloves into the orange to make a Halloween face.
3. Display your Jack-o-Orange for everyone to see.

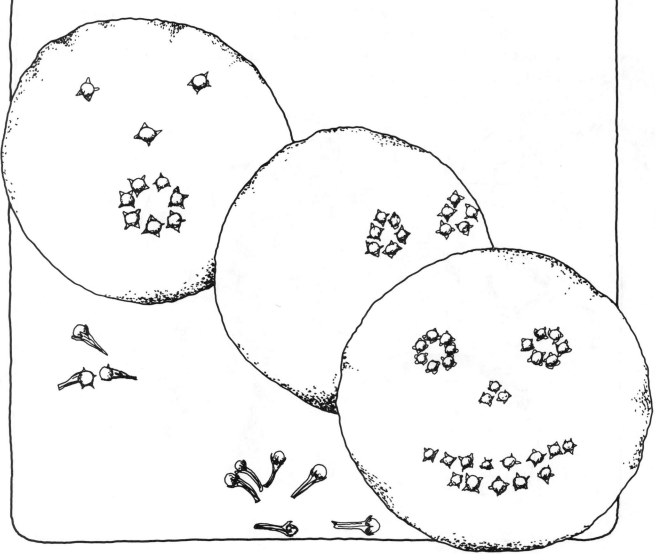

Halloween Paper Bag Mask

You Will Need:
large paper bag
scissors
non-toxic felt-tip pens, crayons, or paints
glue
feathers, glitter, pipe cleaners, tissue paper, etc.

What You Do:
1. Place the bag over your head and feel where your eyes and mouth are.
2. Mark these places with a crayon or marker or have a friend do it for you.
3. Take the bag off and cut out the places you marked. These holes will be for your eyes and mouth.
4. Decorate the mask to look like any creature you like.
5. Put your mask on and let your friends try to guess who or what you are.

Paper Plate Mask

You Will Need:
paper plate
non-toxic felt-tip pens
scissors
plastic spoon
tissue paper, construction paper, feathers, glitter, sequins, felt
    scraps, etc.

What You Do:
1. Hold the plate to your face and ask a friend to mark where your eyes and mouth are.
2. Cut out the holes where the marks are.
3. Decide what character you want to be and design your plate to look that way.
4. Glue the back of the spoon to the bottom of the plate so the handle sticks out beyond the plate. Wait for the glue to dry.
5. Using the spoon as a handle, hold up your mask and let your friends guess who or what you are.

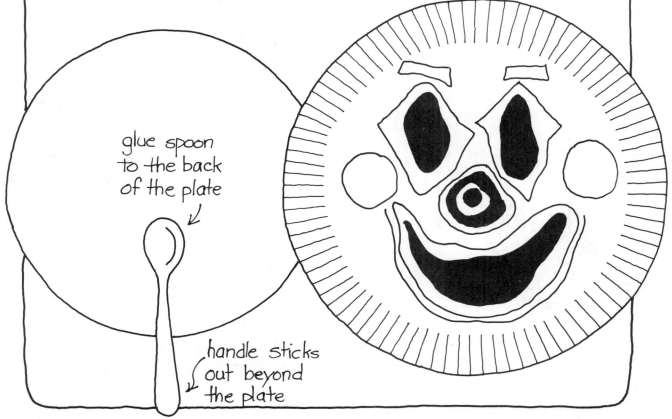

glue spoon to the back of the plate

handle sticks out beyond the plate

Thanksgiving

The Thanksgiving Game

April Fools' Day
We like for its pranks.
But why, you may wonder,
Have a day just for thanks?

To discover the answer,
Simply try to recall
What's good in your life.
List things big and things small.

If you spend a few minutes
On this game of thanks giving,
You'll learn being thankful
Makes life more worth living.

Thanksgiving Turkey Collage

You Will Need:
construction paper
non-toxic felt-tip pen or pencil
glue
different types of uncooked macaroni and beans

What You Do:
1. Place your hand with your fingers spread out on a piece of construction paper.
2. Trace around your hand with a felt-tip pen or pencil.
3. Use the pen or pencil to draw turkey feet at the bottom of the hand you drew. Draw an eye on the thumb.
4. Decorate the turkey by gluing on beans and macaroni.

Popcorn Corsage

You Will Need:
popped popcorn
cardboard circle 3″ in diameter
glue
green pipe cleaner

What You Do:
1. Glue lots of popcorn to the cardboard circle. Make a design or create a free-form shape.
2. Glue the pipe cleaner to the bottom of the circle, near the edge, and curl it around like a plant stem.
3. Wait for glue to dry.
4. Present the corsage to a Thanksgiving Pilgrim or wear it in your own buttonhole.

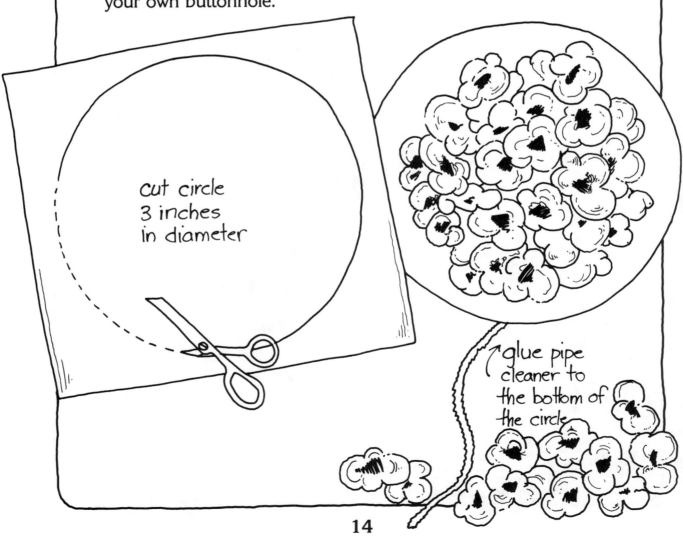

cut circle
3 inches
in diameter

glue pipe
cleaner to
the bottom of
the circle

Cup-o-Turkey

You Will Need:
paper cup
½ of a paper plate
glue
non-toxic felt-tip pens
feathers (optional)

What You Do:
1. Stand the cup on its rim, upside down, and spread glue along one side.
2. Glue the half paper plate, flat side down, to the side of the cup.
3. Draw a turkey face on the front of the cup with the pens.
4. Glue feathers to the plate to become the tail.
5. Put the turkey in the center of your Thanksgiving dinner table for a delightful decoration.

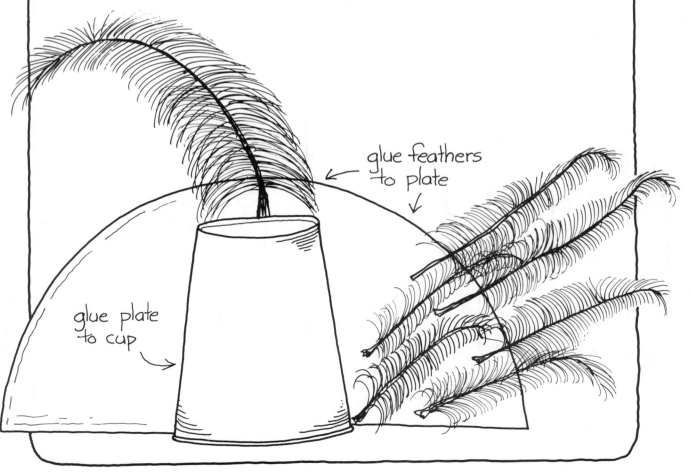

glue feathers to plate

glue plate to cup

Chanukah

The Festival of Lights

Most holidays are one day long,
But Chanukah lasts for eight.
"The Festival of Lights," it's called.
A time to celebrate.
At first—a single candle.
Then two on the second night.
One by one they're added
Until all burn so bright.

Chanukah Pencil Dreidle

You Will Need:
egg carton
pencil
scissors
glue
sequins and/or glitter
paper

What You Do:
1. Cut the egg carton into 12 separate egg holders.
2. Poke a hole through the bottom of each egg holder.
3. Decorate as many egg holders as you like with sequins and glitter.
4. After the decorations have dried stick a sharpened pencil through the hole in one of the holders.
5. Put a piece of paper under your dreidle, then twirl the pencil. See the neat picture it makes!

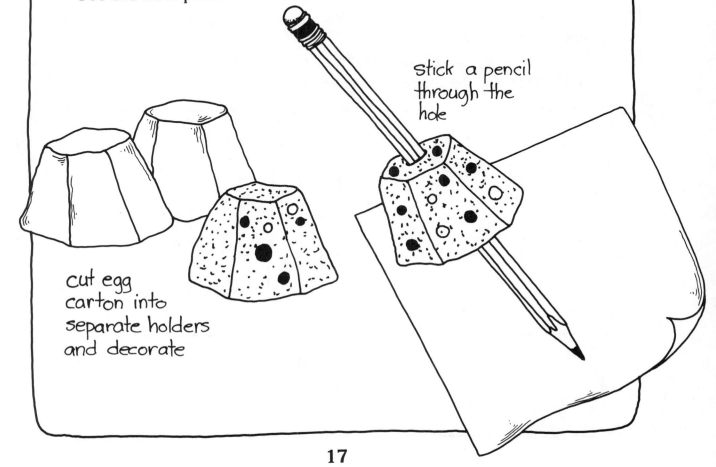

cut egg carton into separate holders and decorate

stick a pencil through the hole

Chanukah Torah Card

You Will Need:
2 round clothespins
construction paper
scissors
glue or paste
non-toxic felt-tip pens

What You Do:
1. Cut the construction paper into a strip whose width is a little shorter than the length of a clothespin.
2. Glue a clothespin to each end of the strip.
3. While you're waiting for the glue to dry, cut out nine small strips of construction paper for candles.
4. Cut out or tear little scraps of paper for flames.
5. When the glue has dried, glue the paper candles in a row between the clothespins. Glue the paper flames to the top of the candles.
6. Draw a base under the candles with the felt-tip pens. Now you have a menorah.
7. When everything is dry, roll the clothespins toward each other.
8. Present the Torah card to a friend on Chanukah.

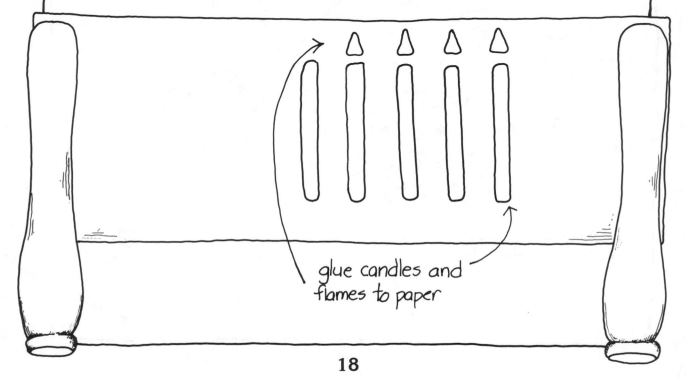

glue candles and flames to paper

Star of David Ornament

You Will Need:
2 pipe cleaners
glue
glitter
yarn

What You Do:
1. Bend each pipe cleaner into a triangle. Twist the ends together.
2. Spread glue on one side of each triangle and place one upside down on the other. Press and let dry.
3. Dab glue onto the star and sprinkle on glitter.
4. Thread a length of yarn through the center, knot the ends, and hang your sparkling star from the top of a window.

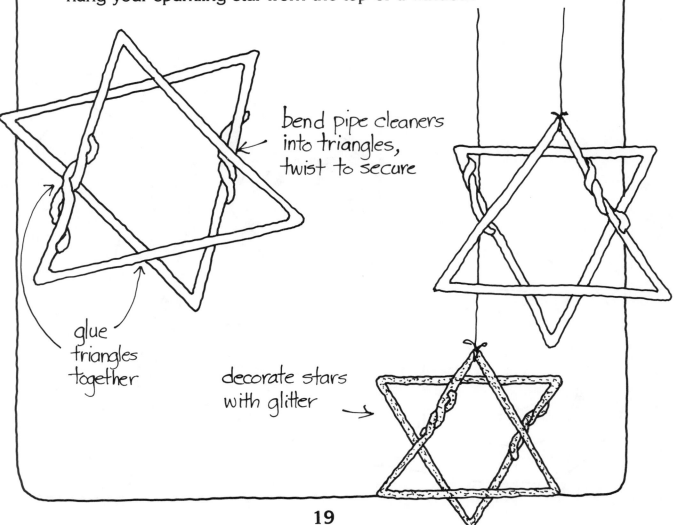

bend pipe cleaners into triangles, twist to secure

glue triangles together

decorate stars with glitter

Christmas

The Words Santa Likes to Hear

One day while he fixed up his sled,
To the elves here's what Santa Claus said,
"When I hear the word *gimme*,
Gimme, gimme, gimme, gimme,
I wish I were back in my bed.

"How much nicer it sounds when I hear,
Friendly wishes for holiday cheer.
When folks busy as bees,
Say *thank you* and *please*
Then I'm happy that Christmas is near."

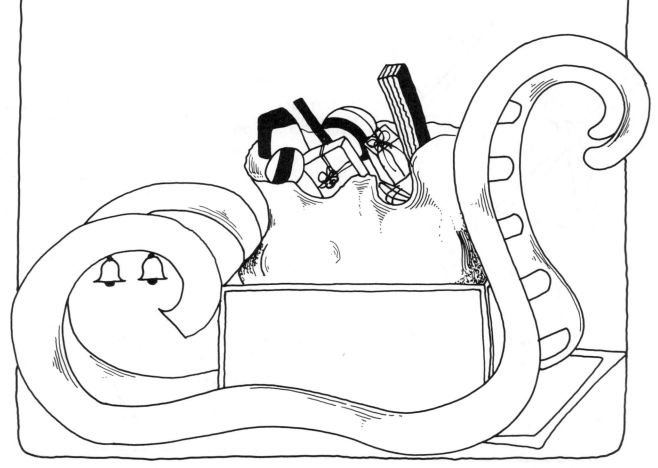

Christmas Noisemaker

You Will Need:
clear plastic cup
popped popcorn
glue
uncooked white beans
paper plate
pen or pencil

What You Do:
1. Trace the top of the cup onto the paper plate.
2. Cut out the circle you traced. Check to see that it is not smaller than the top of the cup.
3. Put some beans and popcorn inside the cup.
4. Spread glue around the edges of the paper circle and place it on top of the cup. Press the circle and cup together for a few seconds to make sure the glue sticks.
5. After the glue has dried hold up your noisemaker and shake, rattle, and roll.

cut circle out and
spread rim
with glue

fill cup with
popcorn and beans

Christmas Wreath

You Will Need:
paper plate
3"-4" squares of red and green tissue paper
glue
scissors
yarn

What You Do:
1. Cut out a good-sized circle in the middle of the paper plate. The plate may have an indented circle to follow.
2. Make tissue flowers by putting your finger inside a green square and wrapping it around your finger. Glue them to the paper plate. Cover the entire wreath with flowers.
3. Add berries to the wreath by gluing on bits of red tissue.
4. Now string yarn through the center of the wreath and hang it from a door or wear it as a necklace.

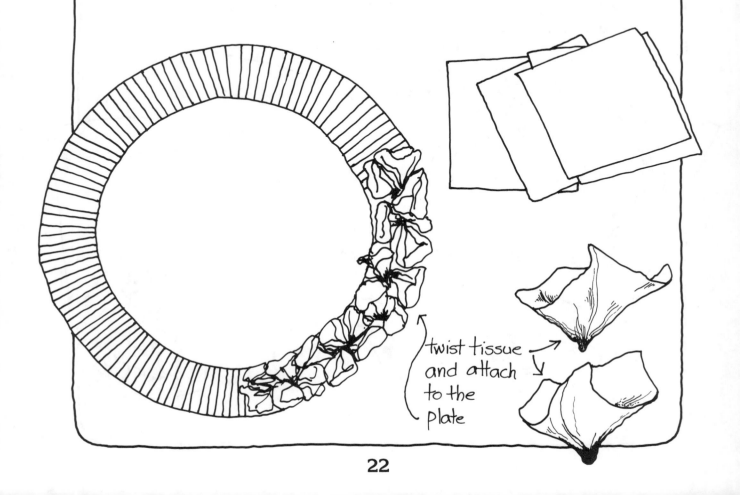

twist tissue and attach to the plate

Macaroni Ornament

You Will Need:
wagon wheel macaroni
glue
scissors
construction paper
wax paper
yarn

What You Do:
1. Place a large piece of wax paper over the work area.
2. Pour a small quantity of glue onto a corner of the wax paper.
3. Dip pieces of macaroni in the glue and stick them together in the shape of a snowflake.
4. Cut out a circle of construction paper at least as big as the snowflake and glue the snowflake to it.
5. After the glue dries, pierce a hole in the top of the construction paper circle and thread yarn through it.
6. The snowflake is ready to be worn as a necklace—by you or your Christmas tree.

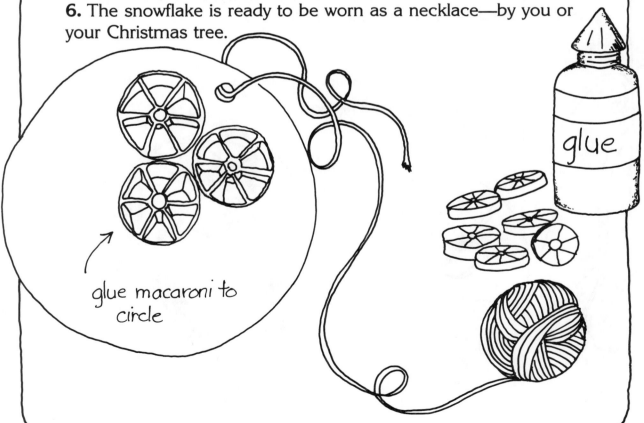

glue macaroni to circle

glue

Christmas Bells

You Will Need:
Styrofoam cup or a cut-out section from an egg carton
small jingle bells
glue
scissors
yarn
foil, glitter, sequins, tinsel, tissue paper, construction paper, pens,
    paints, etc.

What You Do:
1. Use the scissors to punch a hole in the flat base of the cup.
2. Tie a knot at the end of a piece of yarn. Thread the yarn through the hole so the knot is inside the cup. The cup should dangle upside down.
3. Glue one jingle bell to the yarn knot.
4. Decorate the outside of the cup, using tinsel, paper, glitter, etc.
5. Hang the Christmas bell on a tree or on the front door. If you make several bells, bunch them together.

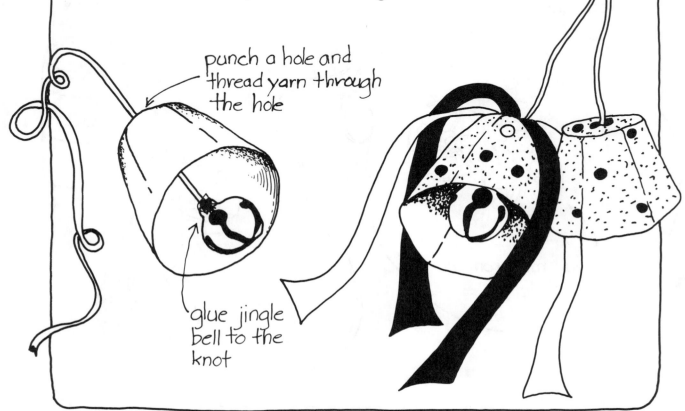

punch a hole and thread yarn through the hole

glue jingle bell to the knot

3D Christmas Card

You Will Need:
construction paper
scissors
doilies
tissue paper
glue or paste
glitter and/or sequins
straws

What You Do:
1. Choose a piece of construction paper for the background.
2. Cut out Christmas tree-shaped triangles from a different color of construction paper.
3. Paste or glue the trees to the background.
4. Glue a section of a straw to the base of each tree for the tree trunk.
5. Cut doilies apart and paste them under and next to the trees to look like snowdrifts.
6. Decorate the trees and the sky with glitter and sequins for a beautiful Christmas Eve.

Christmas Star Card

You Will Need:
tissue paper
construction paper
straws (the short ones used for stirring coffee work best)
glue
glitter
scissors

What You Do:
1. Glue a circle of tissue paper onto a piece of construction paper.
2. Glue the straws to the tissue circle in the shape of a star (cut the straws as needed).
3. Use the glitter to decorate the Christmas star.

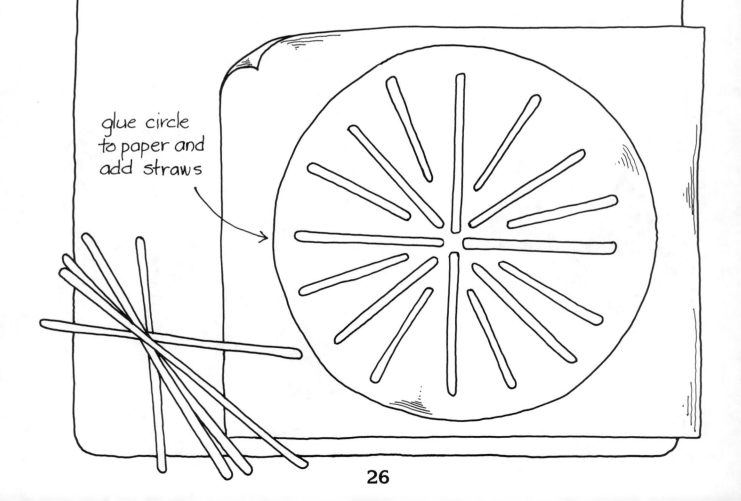

glue circle to paper and add straws

Christmas Cloves

You Will Need:
green tissue paper
red ribbon or pipe cleaner
whole cloves
string (optional)

What You Do:
1. Put a handful of cloves onto a piece of tissue paper.
2. Lift up the ends of the tissue paper and tie them together with a length of ribbon or a pipe cleaner.
3. Now either add a loop of string to the top of the bag and hang it from your Christmas tree, or put the bag in a drawer to make your clothes smell delicious!

New Year's Day

The First Day of the Year

Everyone has a birthday,
I have one and so do you.
But did you ever notice
Each year has a birthday, too?

This birthday has a special name.
We call it New Year's Day.
And everyone's invited
To cheer and eat and play.

That's why each January,
On the day that's number one,
You'll see most people smiling,
Ringing bells and having fun.

Party Hat

You Will Need:
construction paper
scissors
glue or paste
stapler or tape
tissue paper
feathers, ribbons, yarn, etc.

What You Do:
1. Cut three 12″-long strips of construction paper.
2. Staple or tape two of the strips at one end. Fit them around your head and staple or tape the ends together to make a headband.
3. Staple or tape the third strip of paper over the headband from one side to the other to reinforce it.
4. Turn the headband into a party hat with strips of tissue paper, feathers, ribbon curlicues, etc.
5. Wear the hat to a dress-up party.

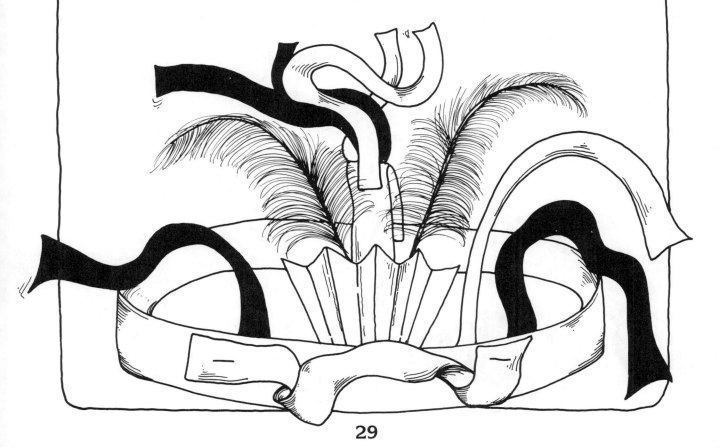

New Year's Day Noisemakers

You Will Need:
Styrofoam cup
glue
plastic spoon
lightweight cardboard
scissors
tissue paper, glitter, construction paper, ribbon, etc.
beans, beads, macaroni, or other noisemakers

What You Do:
1. Decorate the cup with glitter or other materials and let it dry.
2. Fill the cup approximately one fourth full with beans or other noisemakers.
3. Cut a square of cardboard that will cover the top of the cup.
4. Make a hole in the center of the square just big enough for the spoon handle to fit through. Stick in the spoon handle. If the hole is too large, fold a small piece of construction paper and glue it in the hole.
5. Glue the cardboard square to the cup with the handle sticking out. Let the glue dry.
6. Hold the handle and shake it to make noise!!

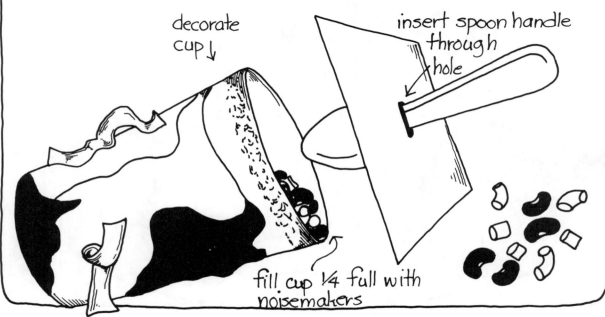

decorate cup ↓

insert spoon handle through hole

fill cup ¼ full with noisemakers

Paper Plate Shaker

You Will Need:
2 paper plates
glue
scissors
glitter, construction paper, beads, sequins, yarn, etc.
uncooked beans and macaroni

What You Do:
1. Put the beans and macaroni onto one of the paper plates.
2. Spread glue around the edges of both plates and press the plates together for 20 seconds or longer.
3. Let the glue dry, then decorate the plates as you like.
4. Use one hand or two to shake up a storm.

This shaker can also be made with aluminum pie plates instead of paper plates.

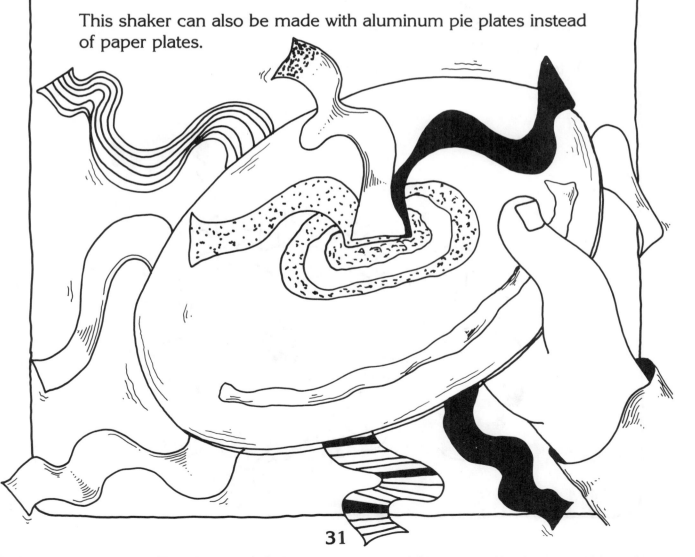

Valentine's Day

A New Kind of Valentine

One afternoon not long ago,
As Valentine's Day drew near,
There was an angry meeting of
Foot, Nose, Arm, Eye, and Ear.

"Why," they asked, "should Valentines
Be covered just with hearts?
Wouldn't it be much fairer
To use some other parts?"

If you agree, here's what to do,
To give your friends some grins.
Try drawing this year's cards
With eyes or mouths or toes or chins,
Or tongues or elbows or knees or . . .

Valentine Doily

You Will Need:
doily
non-toxic felt-tip pens
pipe cleaners
glue

What You Do:
1. Bend the pipe cleaner into a heart shape.
2. Glue the heart to a doily.
3. Color in the heart with pens.
4. Give the Valentine Doily to your sweetheart.

Foil Heart

You Will Need:
construction paper
foil
glue
scissors
non-toxic felt-tip pens

What You Do:
1. Fold a sheet of construction paper in half.
2. Trace or draw half a heart shape on the folded edge of the paper and cut it out.
3. Open the paper. There will be a complete cut-out heart in the middle.
4. Glue a piece of foil to one side of the paper, covering the hole where the heart was cut out.
5. Draw hearts or other designs on the paper around the foil heart. Keep this card or give it to your sweetheart.

fold paper, trace heart and cut

foil

Broken-Hearted Valentine

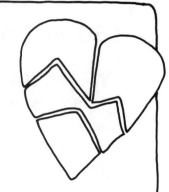

You Will Need:
construction paper
glue
scissors
envelope

What You Do:
1. Glue two sheets of different-colored construction paper together.
2. Wait for the glue to dry.
3. Fold the glued paper in half. Then trace or draw half a heart using the crease for the one straight edge. (See Foil Heart.)
4. Cut around the outline and open up the heart. You should have a valentine with a different color on each side.
5. Cut the heart into four large pieces.
6. Put the pieces into an envelope and let a friend try and mend your broken heart.

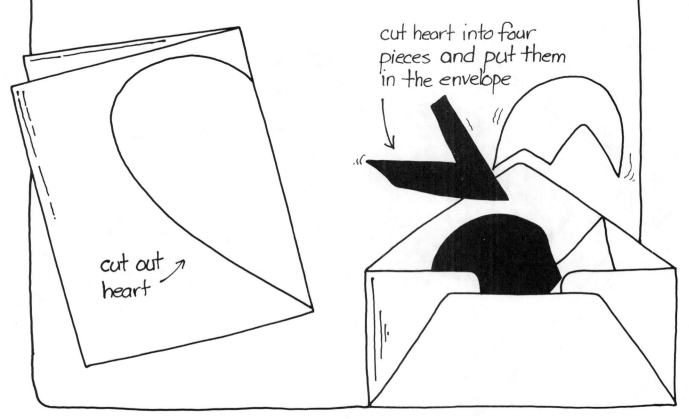

cut heart into four pieces and put them in the envelope

cut out heart

Sweet-Smelling Jello Valentine

You Will Need:
1 package red Jello (raspberry, cherry, or strawberry)
water
construction paper
paintbrush

What You Do:
1. Mix Jello with enough water to form a thickish paste.
2. Paint a heart on a piece of construction paper with the Jello paste.
3. Let the valentine dry. This may take overnight.
4. Give your fragrant raspberry heart to the sweetest Valentine you know.

Sticky Scented Valentine

You Will Need:
1 package red Jello (raspberry, cherry, or strawberry)
glue
construction paper
paintbrush

What You Do:
1. Use the glue to draw a heart on your construction paper.
2. Sprinkle powdered Jello on the glue to make it red.
3. Shake off excess Jello.
4. Let your valentine dry.
5. Send it to someone special.

paint heart with brush and glue and dust with Jello

St. Patrick's Day

Wearing of the Green

On St. Patrick's Day
I've always been seen,
Like most of my friends,
Wearing clothing that's green.

I've worn green knee socks,
Green pants with green belt.
Why, one year I had on
A cap of green felt.

But this year I'm thinking,
It might be a treat,
If the green thing I wear
Were something to eat.

Some green olive jewelry
Might work with some fruit—
Would a green onion ring
Match a green, apple-peel suit?

You'll have to agree
That my idea's a winner.
Who else will wear something
That tastes good for dinner?

St. Patrick's Day Shamrock Wand

You Will Need:
green construction paper
3″-diameter cardboard circle or plastic lid
drinking straw
scissors
glue
glitter
pencil

What You Do:
1. Draw three circles on the green construction paper by tracing around the lid or cardboard.
2. Cut out the circles.
3. Glue together a section of the circles' edges to form a clover shape.
4. Dab glue onto the shamrock and sprinkle on glitter.
5. Glue the top of the straw to the back of the base of the clover.
6. After the glue dries, see how much St. Patrick's Day magic the shamrock wand can create.

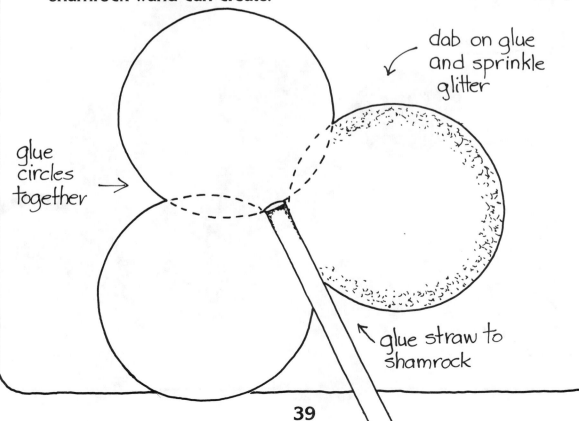

dab on glue and sprinkle glitter

glue circles together →

↖ glue straw to shamrock

Green Potato Press Picture

You Will Need:
½ of an uncooked potato
a tin or foil bowl of green paint
construction paper
non-toxic felt-tip markers

What You Do:
1. Dip the cut surface of the potato into the green paint.
2. Press the potato anywhere you like on the construction paper.
3. Keep dipping and pressing until the paper is covered with green shapes.
4. Wait for the paint to dry, and either hang up the picture or draw on it with non-toxic felt-tip markers.

← dip in green paint and press on paper →

St. Patrick's Day Collage

You Will Need:
construction paper
green non-toxic felt-tip pen
glue
green sequins, felt scraps, beads, glitter, etc.

What You Do:
1. Draw a St. Patrick's Day picture on a sheet of construction paper.
2. Fill any spaces in the picture with green sequins or other decorations.
3. Let your green St. Patrick's Day collage dry, and then hang it on a wall for viewing.

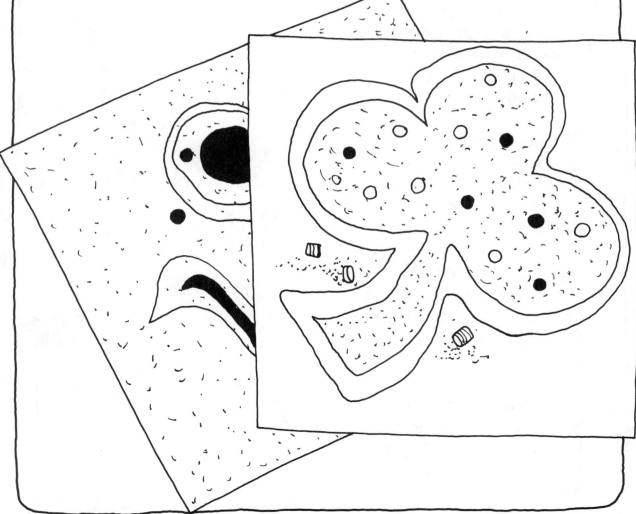

April Fools' Day

'Twas the First Day of April

(Children shout "April Fool" at the end of each stanza.)
'Twas the first day of April,
And all through the school,
Everybody was playing
The game of April Fool.
April Fool!

Our teacher had brought
Her pet parrot this day,
And told us to learn
All the bird had to say.
April Fool!

At lunch the cook told us,
"I'm serving hot soup,
Made of mushrooms and spinach
Plus liver and gloop."
April Fool!

The nurse told us candy
Was what we should eat,
If we wanted to grow up
As tall as six feet.
April Fool!

The day was such fun,
With jokes as you've heard,
Of course, we didn't learn much
From teacher's pet bird.
April Fool!

Now, maybe tomorrow
We'll learn something new,
Because no one tells jokes
When the date's April 2.
April Fool!

April Fools' Jack-in-the-Cup

You Will Need:
Styrofoam cup
plastic spoon
paper nut cup or single section from an egg carton
pens or poster paints and a brush
tissue paper cut into strips
glue
scissors

What You Do:
1. Give your egg holder or nut cup a face and tissue paper hair and wait for it to dry.
2. Dip the bowl end of the spoon in glue and glue a wad of tissue paper to it.
3. Dip the end of the tissue paper wad in glue and stick it inside the nut cup or egg holder head.
4. After the glue dries, make a hole the size of the spoon handle in the bottom of the Styrofoam cup.
5. Make your Jack-in-the-Cup go up and down by pushing the spoon handle up and down.
6. Ask a friend if he or she wants a drink from your cup and . . . April Fool!!

push spoon
handle up and
pull down

April Fools' Day Upside-Down Card

You Will Need:
construction paper
non-toxic felt-tip markers

What You Do:
1. Fold a sheet of construction paper in half to make a greeting card.
2. Draw a picture with the markers on the front half of the construction paper card.
3. Open the card and turn it upside down. Draw another picture.
4. Give the card to a friend on April first and watch the surprised look when the card is opened.

April Funnies

You Will Need:
Sunday newspaper comics
construction paper
glue
scissors

What You Do:
1. Cut out a number of different frames from the comic strips.
2. Organize the frames into a story and glue them to a piece of construction paper.
3. Give a friend this April Fools' Day card and see if he or she can decipher your wacky story.

Easter

The Easter Egg Surprise

When I sat down to paint an egg,
For Easter, first came blue.
Then I dipped my brush in pink,
And red and silver, too.

I painted birds and flowers,
Near a tiny wishing well.
Plus dogs and cats and children
All around that pretty shell.

But before I had a chance to let
My friends take one quick peek,
The egg went "crack" and then I saw
A pointed yellow beak.

"Stop!" I shouted. "Go back in.
You'll ruin my Easter egg."
The chick said only, "Peep, peep, peep,"
And pushed out one thin leg.

So now I have no painted egg,
Which makes me almost sad.
But when I hear that "Peep, peep, peep,"
I know the chick is glad.

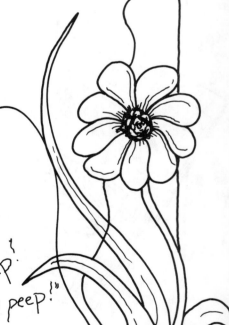

"peep!
peep peep!"

Easter Basket

You Will Need:

small plastic or cardboard basket (the kind used to hold cherry
    tomatoes and berries)
doily
colored tissue paper
2 pipe cleaners
paste or glue

What You Do:

1. Tear a small square of tissue paper, then form a flower by
putting your finger in the center of the square and wrapping the
excess tissue around it.
2. Make 10 or 12 flowers, then glue them to the outside of the
basket.
3. Line the inside of the basket with the doily or tissue paper.
4. Take the pipe cleaners and twist them together into one long
piece. Fasten the ends to opposite sides of the basket for a
handle.
5. When the glue on the flowers has dried, the Easter basket is
ready for egg hunting.

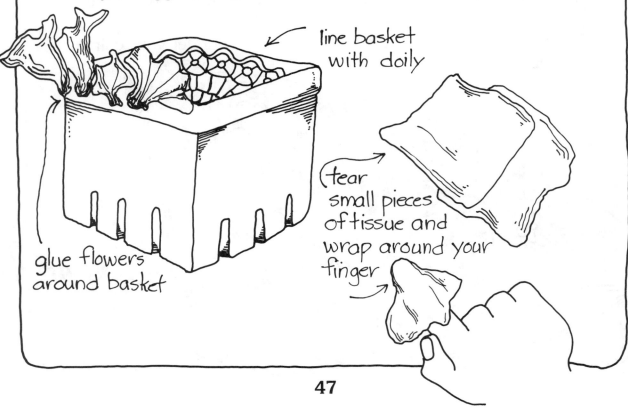

line basket
with doily

glue flowers
around basket

tear
small pieces
of tissue and
wrap around your
finger

Easter Bonnet

You Will Need:
paper plate
colored tissue paper
doilies
glue
scissors
yarn
hole punch

What You Do:
1. Choose a piece of tissue paper and glue it to the underside of the paper plate. Turn the plate over.
2. After the glue dries, trim the edges of the tissue paper so that none hangs over the plate.
3. Glue one or more doilies on top of the tissue paper.
4. While the doilies are drying, choose some different colors of tissue paper and make a number of tissue flowers (see page 56 for directions).
5. When you have as many flowers as you want, glue them to the paper plate in any design you like.
6. When the glue has dried, punch a hole on each side of the plate and string a piece of yarn through the holes.
7. Now slip on your Easter bonnet, tie a bow under your chin, and parade.

glue flowers to hat

Easter Egg Necklace

You Will Need:
several colors of construction paper
scissors
hole punch
yarn
glue
glitter
sequins
non-toxic felt-tip markers

What You Do:
1. Cut several oval (egg-shaped) pieces out of different colors of construction paper.
2. Punch a hole in the edge of each egg.
3. Decorate the Easter eggs with non-toxic felt-tip markers, glitter, sequins, etc.
4. Thread a length of yarn through the eggs and knot the ends to make a necklace.
5. Slip on the Easter necklace and start hunting for the Easter Bunny!!

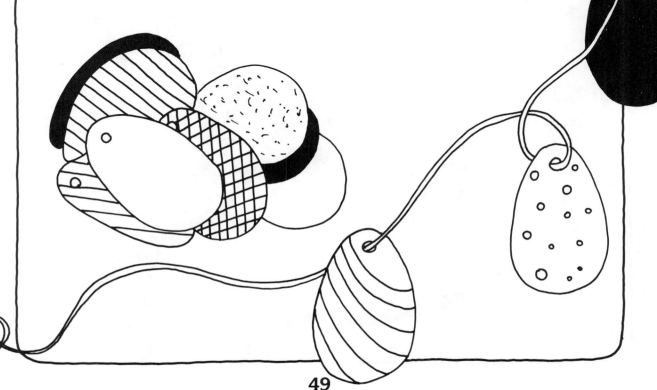

Egg Carton Tulips

You Will Need:
egg carton
pipe cleaners
paste or glue
tissue paper
scissors
paints and brushes or non-toxic felt-tip pens

What You Do:
1. Cut the carton into 12 separate egg holders.
2. Cut around the top of each egg holder so that it has a tulip shape.
3. Poke a hole through the bottom of each tulip.
4. Stick a pipe cleaner through each hole and secure by folding the tip over and pasting or gluing it to the inside of the tulip.
5. Decorate the flowers with tissue paper, paints, or pens.
6. Twist the stems together or tie a bow around your tulip.

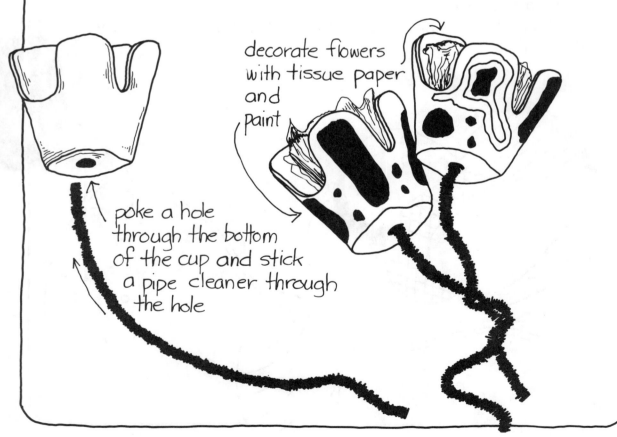

decorate flowers with tissue paper and paint

poke a hole through the bottom of the cup and stick a pipe cleaner through the hole

Easter Bouquet

You Will Need:
paper baking cups
pipe cleaners
scissors
glue
ribbon
glitter

What You Do:
1. Punch a hole with the scissors in the bottom of a baking cup.
2. Stick a pipe cleaner through the hole and bend the top of it over. Glue it in place.
3. Dab glue all over the flower and decorate with glitter.
4. Make three or four more flowers and twist the stems together. Tie the bunch with a ribbon.
5. Show your friends your green thumb on a bright sunny day.

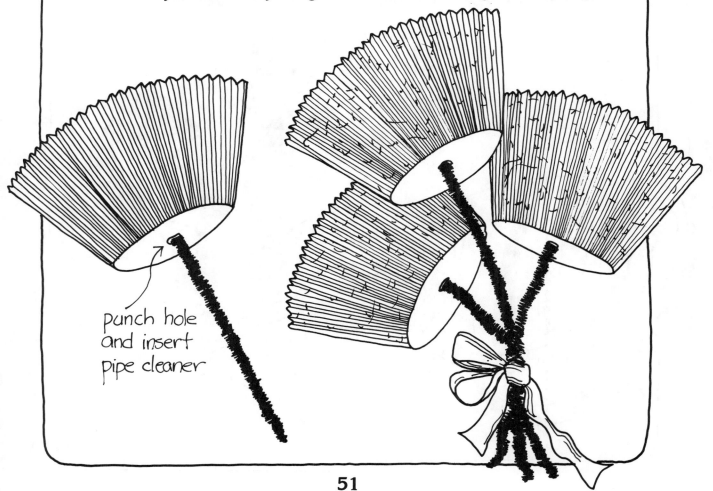

punch hole
and insert
pipe cleaner

Easter Egg Puzzle

You Will Need:
construction paper
scissors
glue
glitter
non-toxic felt-tip markers
envelope

What You Do:
1. Cut out a large oval (egg-shaped) piece from a sheet of construction paper.
2. Decorate the oval with non-toxic felt-tip markers and glitter so it looks like a beautiful Easter egg.
3. Cut the egg into four large pieces.
4. Put the pieces into an envelope and give the envelope to a friend on Easter. See if he or she can turn your puzzle into an egg again.

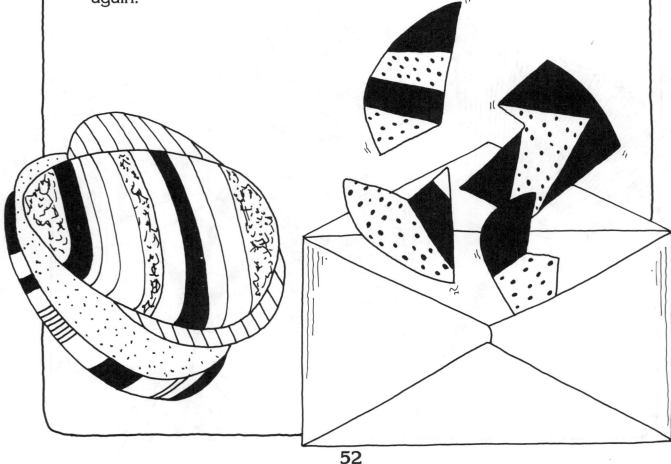

Feel the Easter Bunny

You Will Need:
construction paper
cotton balls
glue
non-toxic felt-tip markers
glitter

What You Do:
1. Glue three cotton balls in the shape of a triangle to a piece of construction paper.
2. Draw two eyes on the top cotton ball and two bunny ears above it, on the construction paper, with a non-toxic felt-tip marker.
3. Surround the bunny with several Easter eggs using markers and glitter.
4. Show your friends your soft Easter bunny—they may want to pet it!

May Day

What May Said to April

"May Day is my day,"
Said May, the month of flowers.
"Of course, they wouldn't be blooming
Without sweet April's showers."

"Thank you, May," said April.
"It's kind of you to say,
That what I do helps set the stage
For a month of outdoor play."

May Day Daffodil

You Will Need:
1″-diameter yellow construction paper circle
egg cup cut from an egg carton
pipe cleaner
scissors
glue
paper doily

What You Do:
1. Glue the yellow circle to the bottom of the egg cup.
2. Poke a hole through the bottom of the egg cup and the circle with the scissors.
3. Stick the pipe cleaner through the hole, then bend the top over and glue it to the inside of the egg cup.
4. Cut the edges off the paper doily and glue them onto the sides of the egg cup to make a frill.
5. Twist the stem of the daffodil to make it curl and give the flower to your buddy on May first.

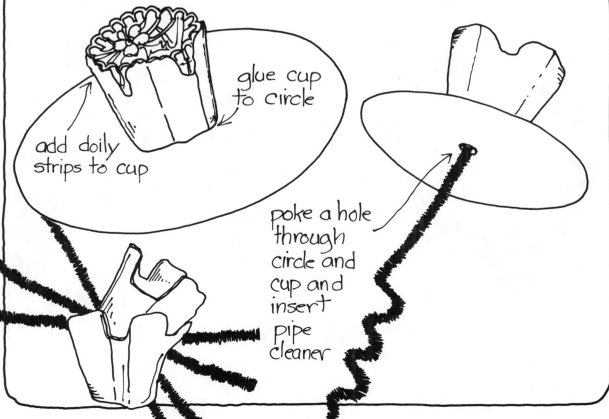

glue cup to circle

add doily strips to cup

poke a hole through circle and cup and insert pipe cleaner

Tissue Flowers

You Will Need:
tissue paper
straws (the small kind used to stir coffee)
glue or paste
scissors

What You Do:
1. Tear or cut small squares of different-colored tissue paper.
2. Place a finger in the center of each square and wrap the excess tissue around it. Make flowers out of all the squares.
3. Dip the end of a straw in glue and wrap the bottom of one flower (where the point of your finger was) around it. Do this for all the flowers.
4. Cut some of the straw stems if you want shorter flowers.
5. Let the flowers dry, then place them in a basket (you could use the one on page 57) and present them to someone you like.

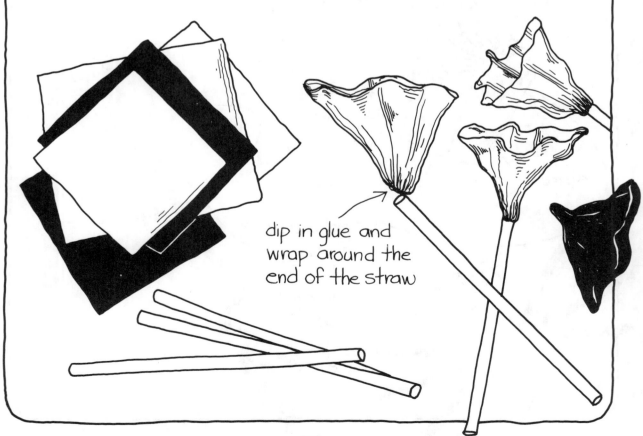

dip in glue and wrap around the end of the straw

Doily Basket

You Will Need:
large doilies
paste

What You Do:
1. Take a doily and fold it into a cone shape.
2. Paste the edge down.
3. Fold the bottom of the doily up and paste it over for a flat bottom.
4. Let the doily dry while you make tissue flowers to go in it.

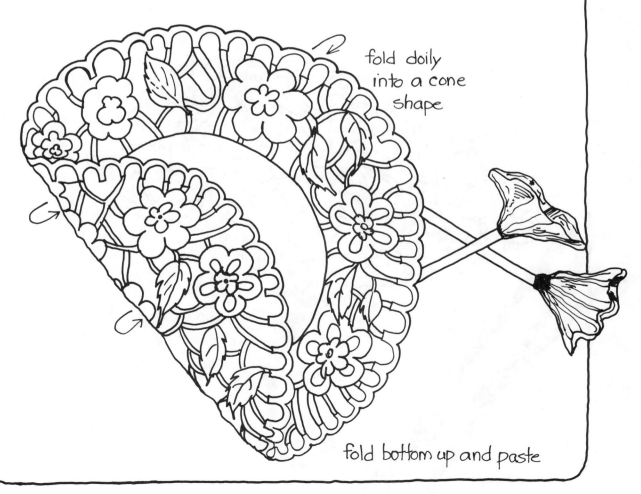

fold doily into a cone shape

fold bottom up and paste

Doily Nosegay

You Will Need:
small doilies
glue
pipe cleaners
ribbon

What You Do:
1. Form a doily into a flower shape.
2. Dip the bottom edge in glue and wrap a pipe cleaner around it, or stick a pipe cleaner through the doily and twist to make a knot.
3. Make four or five doily flowers and tie them together with a ribbon. The nosegay makes a wonderful Mother's Day present or a present to give yourself.

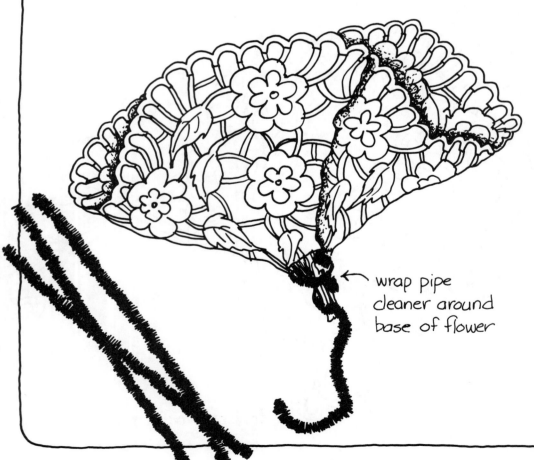

wrap pipe cleaner around base of flower

May Pole

You Will Need:
tissue paper
clay or playdough
straws (the small kind used to stir coffee)
doily or paper plate
paste or glue
scissors

What You Do:
1. Cut or rip strips of different-colored tissue paper.
2. Form a small piece of clay into a base and place a straw upright in the center.
3. Glue the strips of tissue paper to the top of the straw.
4. Glue the May Pole to a doily or paper plate.
5. Take the May Pole outside and watch the tissue paper fly in the breeze.

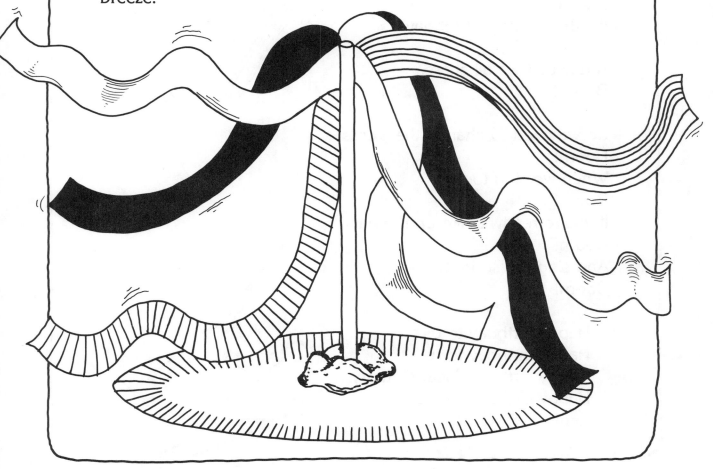

Independence Day

Happy Birthday to Us

(Children can yell "Boom" at the end of each line.)

Up, up goes a rocket.
Boom!
See the sparkles floating down.
Boom!
It's a special party
Boom!
For everyone in town.
Boom!

This day belongs to you and me.
Boom!
There are picnics everywhere.
Boom!
It's the country's birthday.
Boom!
A day that we all share.
Boom!

So we need to change the words
Boom!
When we sing today.
Boom!
If you're ready, strike up the band
Boom!
And sing the song this way:
Boom!

   Happy birthday to us.
   Happy birthday to us.
   Happy birthday, Dear Country.
   Happy birthday to us.
Boom!

Yankee Doodle Dandy (Macaroni Hat)

You Will Need:
construction paper
uncooked macaroni
feathers
glue
non-toxic felt-tip pen

What You Do:
1. Use a felt-tip pen to draw a hat shape on a sheet of construction paper. The hat can be just a rectangle with a line under it for the brim.
2. Glue macaroni all over your hat drawing.
3. When the glue is dry, glue a feather or two to the brim of the hat.
4. Hold up the hat and call it macaroni.

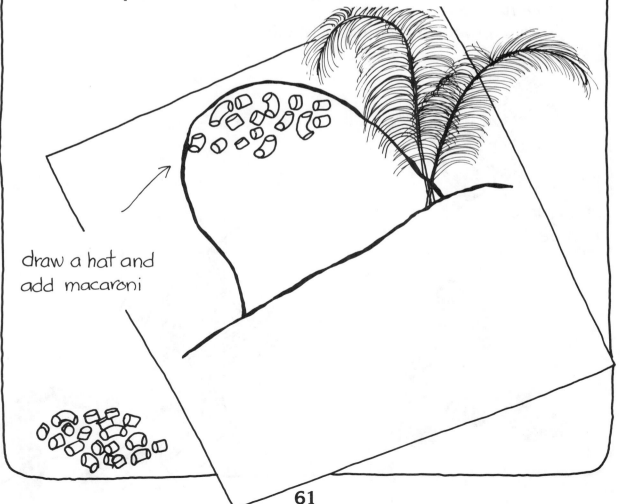

draw a hat and add macaroni

Independence Day Shaker

You Will Need:
toilet paper tube
tissue paper
uncooked beans
scissors
glue
2 nut cups
glitter

What You Do:
1. Glue a nut cup to one end of the toilet paper tube.
2. Pour a handful of beans into the tube.
3. Glue another nut cup to the other end of the tube.
4. Use tissue paper and glitter to make the shaker look like a rocket ship. Strips of paper glued to one end will look like fire streaming from the rocket.
5. Pick up your shaker and blast off!

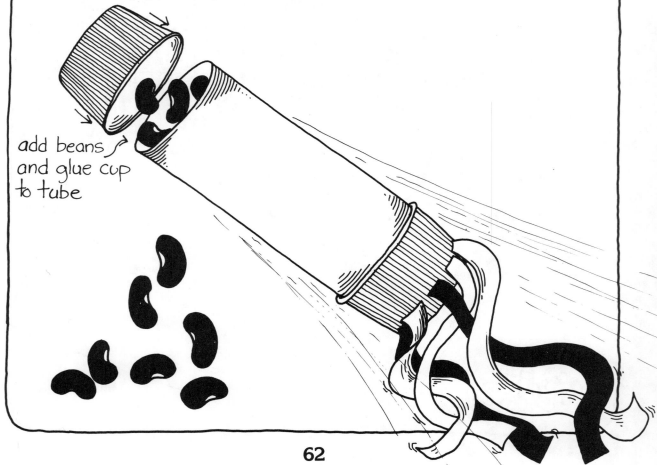

add beans and glue cup to tube

Independence Day Sparkler

You Will Need:
3 pipe cleaners
glue
glitter
scissors

What You Do:
1. Cut two of the pipe cleaners into quarters.
2. Roll the eight pieces in glue and then cover them with glitter.
3. When the glue is dry, glue the glitter-covered pieces onto the third, whole pipe cleaner.
4. Let the sparkling sparkler dry and then wave it in an Independence Day parade!!

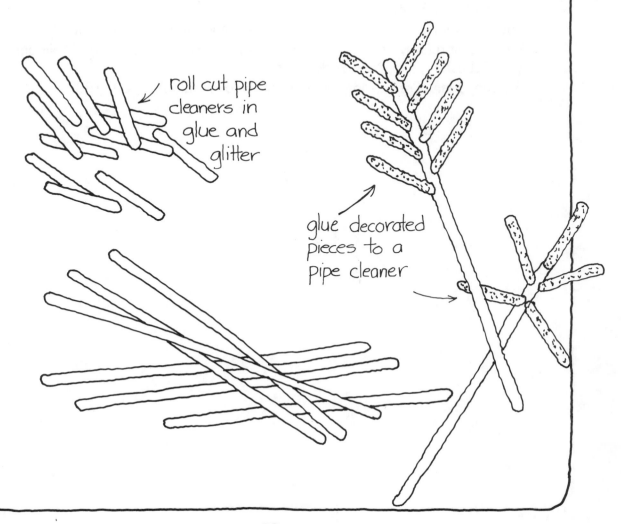

roll cut pipe cleaners in glue and glitter

glue decorated pieces to a pipe cleaner

Resources

Baldwin, Margaret. *Thanksgiving.* Franklin Watts, New York, 1983.

Burns, Marilyn. *The Hanukkah Book.* Four Winds Press, New York, 1981.

Chapman, Jean. *The Sugar Plum Christmas Book.* Children's Press International, Chicago, 1977.

_____ . *Pancakes and Painted Eggs.* Children's Press International, Chicago, 1983.

Cole, Haas, et al. *A Pumpkin in a Pear Tree.* Little, Brown and Co., Boston, 1976.

_____ . *I Saw a Purple Cow.* Little, Brown and Co., Boston, 1972.

Corrigan, Adeline. *Holiday Ring.* Albert Whitman, Chicago, 1975.

Corwin, Judith Hoffman. *Halloween Fun.* Julian Messner, New York, 1983.

Glovach, Linda. *The Little Witch's Halloween Book.* Prentice Hall, Englewood Cliffs, NJ, 1975.

Robinson, Jerri. *Activities for Anyone, Anytime, Anyplace.* Little, Brown and Co., Boston, 1983.

Vaughn, Jenny. *The Easter Book.* Grosset and Dunlap, New York, 1980.

Vermeer and Larivierd. *The Little Kid's Four Seasons Craft Book.* Taplinger Publishing Co., New York, 1974.

Warren, Jean. *Crafts.* Monday Morning Books, Palo Alto, CA, 1983.